Charles Nelan

Cartoons of the war of 1898 with Spain

from leading foreign and American papers

Charles Nelan

Cartoons of the war of 1898 with Spain
from leading foreign and American papers

ISBN/EAN: 9783741152214

Manufactured in Europe, USA, Canada, Australia, Japa

Cover: Foto ©ninafisch / pixelio.de

Manufactured and distributed by brebook publishing software
(www.brebook.com)

Charles Nelan

Cartoons of the war of 1898 with Spain

Cartoons of our war with Spain.

— By —

Chs. Nelan.

FREDERICK A. STOKES COMPANY, PUBLISHERS, NEW YORK

Dedicated to The American People.

Very respectfully yours—

Ch. Nelan

INTRODUCTION

M Y publishers have asked me to write something. This I have already done on every page,—in the picture language, in which alone do I feel that I can do my best. Ten years ago an old German editor in my native State, Ohio, said, " The cartoon will be the editorial of the future."

In this day of American journalistic enterprise, the cartoonist is often called on to make a cartoon in two or three hours and sometimes in less time. Do you wonder that we die young or become paretics?

If we do anything towards moulding public opinion, do not blame us entirely, but remember the editor, whose name does not appear on the cartoon.

I do not believe in the bitter, stinging cartoon. It's always best to produce a laugh with your argument ; people seem to digest it better.

I desire to acknowledge the courtesy of the NEW YORK HERALD in permitting me to publish these cartoons in book form.

CHARLES NELAN,
With the New York Herald.

"*A laugh is worth a hundred groans in any market.*"—LAMB.

KEEP YOUR HEAD COOL.

HE WOULDN'T BE HAPPY UNTIL HE GOT IT.

IT BEGINS TO LOOK AS IF THESE GENTLEMEN AGREED WITH ME.

"WHERE AM I AT?"

"APRIL FOOL!"

A "SHELLING" FOR UNCLE SAM'S EASTER MONDAY.

BEFORE AND AFTER TAKING—RESPONSIBILITY.

"WELL, I'M WAITING NOW."

A SNAP SHOT.

RALLY ROUND THE FLAG.

TAKING HIS PULSE.

BETWEEN TWO FIRES.

THE PRESENT: TO THE STARS AND STRIPES DEWEY OPENED A NEW WORLD.

"DON'T SMILE TILL YOU HEAR FROM SAMPSON."

SPAIN'S DILEMMA.

ALL SIZES AND GOOD FITS FOR ALL THE FAMILY.

NOTICE!

LOST, STRAYED or STOLEN
ONE CAPE VERDE FLEET.
Any one bringing it
to me will be rewar-
ded.

U. S.

SHE'S TUMBLING!

JUST MISSED!

COUSINS.

"WHAT ARE THE WILD WAVES SAYING?"

BOTTLED. WILL HE ESCAPE?

IF THE WAR BRING NOTHING ELSE, WE ARE THANKFUL.

IN
MEMORY
OF
THE HEROES
OF
THE MAINE, SAN JUAN,
CARDENAS, CIENFUEGOS
&c.

THEIR FIRST DECORATION DAY. KEEP THEIR GRAVES GREEN.

"THE CONCERT OF EUROPE."

THE KING'S JESTER.

BLANCO'S MULE STORIES

CERVERA'S REPORTS OF GREAT VICTORIES

SPANISH HUMOR

SPAIN

AND THEN ALONG CAME THE REAL KING.

HE ISN'T HANDSOME, BUT HE COMES HIGH.

WILLIAM, YOU'RE TOO LATE.

U. S.: WELL, THE PATRIOTS ARE NOT ALL IN THE ARMY.

"I WONDER IF HE REALLY WANTS MY WHITE ELEPHANT."

ANNOUNCEMENT EXTRAORDINARY.

TROUBLES WHICH MAY FOLLOW AN IMPERIAL POLICY.

THE BIRTH OF A MARINE GIANT.

"THE BOY STOOD ON THE BURNING DECK."

YOUR ONLY SALVATION.

NOTICE
DON'T MONKEY
WITH THE
BUZZ SAW

THE PHILIPPINES

U.S.

BE CAREFUL.

NERO FIDDLED WHILE ROME BURNED.

EUROPE: "MY GOODNESS, HOW HE IS MUTILATING THAT BEAUTIFUL MAP!"

"GENTLEMEN, AS THE SPANIARD IN THE CAST IS BEHIND IN HIS LINES, THERE WILL
BE A SHORT INTERMISSION."

BEFORE AND AFTER TAKING. UNCLE SAM FREELY TELLS HIS PHYSICIAN THAT HIS
TREATMENT HAS BEEN A SUCCESS.

TWO THINGS HE HAS LEARNED.

THE NEW MEMBER OF THE ORCHESTRA.

THIS ISN'T TOO MUCH FOR A GOOD THING.

UNCLE SAM PAYS THE FREIGHT.

www.ingramcontent.com/pod-product-compliance
Lightning Source LLC
Chambersburg PA
CBHW021526090426
42739CB00007B/808